beholding and becoming

Journals in the Being with God series

an interactive
journal

book four
being with God series

beholding and becoming

*The world is waiting for
a different kind of Christian . . .
Will it be you?*

Graham Cooke

Sovereign World

Sovereign World Ltd
PO Box 777
Tonbridge
Kent TN11 0ZS
England

Requests for information should be addressed to:
Graham Cooke
PO Box 91
Southampton
SO15 5ZE, United Kingdom
Web site: http://www.grahamcooke.com

Unless otherwise indicated, all Scripture quotations are taken from
The Holy Bible, New King James Version. Copyright © 1979, 1980,
1982 by Thomas Nelson, Inc.

ISBN I 85240 371 3

The publishers aim to produce books which will help to extend and
build up the Kingdom of God. We do not necessarily agree with
every view expressed by the author, or with every interpretation of
Scripture expressed. We expect each reader to make his/her
judgement in the light of their own understanding of God's Word
and in an attitude of Christian love and fellowship.

Cover design by CCD, www.ccdgroup.co.uk
Typeset by CRB Associates, Reepham, Norfolk
Printed in the United States of America

dedication

I dedicate this journal to the members of Odyssey, the businessman's spirituality group in California which I co-lead with my great friend Tim Dickerson.

Our times together have been a compelling mixture of grace, search for truth, impacting dialogue, friendship, laughter, and good wine. Thanks!

acknowledgments

I want to thank the journal team of Carole Shiers (my personal assistant), Tim Pettingale (my friend and publisher) and his staff at Sovereign World, and Jordan and Jenny Bateman (editorial). They are a great bunch to work with on a project close to my heart.

Their tireless work, enthusiasm, and unflagging good humour have helped to make this project one of life's great pleasures.

Together, we are all Beholding and Becoming.

beholding and becoming

introduction

You carry a profound and unfathomable call on your life, placed there by God Himself. It is fresh and new and completely beyond your natural ability to accomplish – God has called you to do something you cannot possibly do. You can meditate on that call for the rest of your days, strategize it to no end, even try and seize it; it doesn't matter. Like reaching for the stars, God's call is beyond you. It's a gift God has given each one of His children. In fact, your inability to accomplish it is exactly why He had selected you to carry that call.

As rational human beings, faced with a world bound by goals and measures, we find this difficult to believe. The apostle Paul didn't, however: *"But God has chosen the foolish things of the world to put to shame the wise, and God has chosen the weak things of the world to put to shame the things which are mighty,"* he said in

1 Corinthians 1:27. We are the foolish and the weak Paul referred to – we cannot think our way into fulfilling the call of God. Fortunately, He has not asked us to. God has that covered; His most foolish moment is greater than our wisest and grandest revelation. Paul explained that, too: *"Human wisdom is so tinny, so impotent, next to the seeming absurdity of God. Human strength can't begin to compete with God's 'weakness'"* (1 Corinthians 1:25, The Message). If we cannot grab a hold of this great call, what can we do?

We, as Christians, must learn to live in the consistent nature of God. The Father will never change His heart toward you. Like the father in the story of the Prodigal Son (Luke 15:11–32), He only wants to love His children, no matter the decisions, mistakes or successes they make. When we live in that place of consistency, we get to walk with God into the unpredictable and outrageous. Our lives become an adventure, full of courage and miracles. In the Bible, saints who walked in consistency got to walk on water, see an axhead float, witness the sun standing still in the heavens, raise a child from the dead, and part a river's water. They were pushed by God to a place where even creation obeyed them.

> "It's kind of fun to do the impossible."
> Walt Disney

Creation longs for that breakthrough again. *"For the earnest expectation of the creation eagerly waits for the revealing of the sons of God,''* Paul wrote in Romans 8:19. The landscape of the western world – in the United States, United Kingdom, Canada, Australia, and all points in between – is waiting for a different Christian to emerge from the cozy confines of the Church. A different type of believer is needed. The ground itself longs to see the sons of God, a tribe with the power of the Holy Spirit indwelling their lives, rise up. To them, the experience of the miraculous is largely irrelevant; those mighty works don't matter nearly as much as the One making them possible. Don't walk away from the personhood of God; too many people in the renewal movement of the latter half of the twentieth century did just that. Do the absurd thing – enjoy the experience you're having, but adore the One who is giving it above all else.

We must learn to behold the glory and intimacy of God and become like Him. We need to come into a place of rest where everything that God is can come and touch us. We must stop striving and simply *be*. To fulfill our call, we must be a Mary sitting and waiting at the feet of Jesus, not a Martha running about behind the scenes.

Mary, not Martha

Mary and Martha is a story familiar to many of us. Let's look at it, once again, in Luke 10:38–42:

Now it happened as they went that He entered a certain village; and a certain woman named Martha welcomed Him into her house. And she had a sister called Mary, who also sat at Jesus' feet and heard His word. But Martha was distracted with much serving, and she approached Him and said, "Lord, do You not care that my sister has left me to serve alone? Therefore tell her to help me."

And Jesus answered and said to her, "Martha, Martha, you are worried and troubled about many things. But one thing is needed, and Mary has chosen that good part, which will not be taken away from her."

In our western thinking, we prize activity more than anything else. We feel we always have to be doing something – waking up, walking the dog, driving the kids, teaching Sunday school, picking up the kids, cooking dinner, cutting the lawn, waxing the car, and on and on and on. We are a whirlwind of activity, just like Martha, getting ourselves worked up over everything. Mary, meanwhile, seems lazy to us. Where is the measurable fruit from her day? What has she contributed? Why won't she help her sister serve this important houseguest? Mary's conduct is foreign to our thinking.

Yet it is Mary whom Jesus commends; her rest has served her well. Mary was being consistent in her relationship with Jesus. The biggest desire in God's heart is inhabitation. If you search through Scripture, you'll find that coming and living with His children is all He has ever wanted. All we ever pray for, though, is another move of God.

revival shows our weakness

Unlike inhabitation, there is no call for revival found anywhere in Scripture. The Church, quite simply, should never need reviving. Revival is not about getting people saved; revival is about the Church coming back to her original purpose before God. I think it's very sad that so many of us have prayed and longed for revival – it means the Church is a long way from what God wants us to be. Maybe, just maybe, a little touch from God could bring us immediately into line. That's the mystery of life with the Godhead – you just never know what could turn the tide of history.

> "I believe that the imperative need of the day is not simply revival, but a radical reformation that will go to the root of our moral and spiritual maladies and deal with causes rather than with consequences, with the disease rather than the symptoms."
> A.W. Tozer

We see this in our own lives quite often. One day we're yearning for something, and the next day that thing is fulfilled. How on earth did that happen? What swung the hinge so quickly? It was simply Jesus, coming to inhabit something. This is one of the deep things of God, one of those spiritual mysteries, that is hidden, waiting to be revealed. The gospel writers recorded that Jesus did not trust what was in the hearts of men; my prayer is that God would trust us enough to show us – and do – something new.

For me, revival can be defined as the Church coming back to a place where God can trust us with the things He really wants to give us. When that happens, there will be a reformation; a move of God where the walls of the Church will be knocked flat, and what we have in the meeting is what we have in the marketplace. Miracles will happen, God will be in full evidence, people will get saved by the hundreds and thousands, and creation's longing for the sons of God to move in power will be answered.

living water

To experience this move of God, we must let Jesus inhabit us. We must drink of His living water, as He described in John 7:37–38: *"On the last day, that great day of the feast, Jesus stood and cried out, saying, 'If anyone thirsts, let him come to Me and drink. He who believes in Me, as the Scripture has said, out of his heart will flow rivers of living water.'"* If we are thirsty to fulfill the impossible call of God, we need to drink in Christ's love, allowing Him to fully inhabit our lives.

Water is an allegory Jesus used several times in His ministry to explain His effect on the earth. In John 4,

He met a woman at a well, and told her, *"If you knew the gift of God, and who it is who says to you, 'Give Me a drink,' you would have asked Him, and He would have given you living water"* (John 4:10). He later added that *"whoever drinks of the water that I shall give him will never thirst. But the water that I shall give him will become in him a fountain of water springing up into everlasting life"* (John 4:14). Inhabitation fulfills us at the deepest level, dividing what is our soul – our mind, will, and emotions – from our spirit – our conscience and ability to commune with God. Jesus, whom the apostle John also referred to as the Word of God, splits our spiritual being from our soulish behavior. *"For the word of God is living and powerful, and sharper than any two-edged sword, piercing even to the division of soul and spirit, and of joints and marrow, and is a discerner of the thoughts and intents of the heart,"* Paul wrote in Hebrews 4:12. We must learn how to keep these two things apart, and how to teach our soul to be a vehicle to the movement of our spirit.

> "When we remain in the spirit, we abide in Christ, and Christ has the ground to abide in us to carry out His divine dispensing in us."
> Watchman Nee

be renewed

This process is called being renewed. *"Therefore we do not lose heart. Even though our outward man is perishing, yet the inward man is being renewed day by* day," Paul wrote in 2 Corinthians 4:16. We have been saved, we are being saved, we will be saved. Salvation is one thing; conversion is another. Many Christians just stop with salvation but we are called to be converted into the image of Jesus. Salvation without conversion isn't going to get us anywhere, because life is a journey. We need to learn how to be transformed and conformed to the nature of God. Life is not about coming to Christ, it's about becoming Christ-like.

If God lives in you, you are in the presence of God. What a starting point! God is in me, and I am in the presence of God. God is in you, and you are in the presence of God. We can live that way. When you come into a quiet time, relax – you're in God's presence. Allow the Holy Spirit to develop your patience when it comes to your quiet times. Let Him discipline that part of your nature, conforming it to the example we have in Jesus, a Man who would spend forty days fasting, who would pray all night, and who would wait on His Father. Patience and peace is difficult sometimes, but remember Paul's words: *"I can do all things through Christ who strengthens me"* (Philippians 4:13). Devotion is about being, not about doing. It's about being Mary, not Martha. There's no place for us to rush to; we're already there. God is in us, and we are in the presence of God.

> Life is not about coming to Christ, it's about becoming Christ-like.

The Caim – an ancient Celtic prayer

Christ be with me
Christ within me
Christ behind me
Christ before me
Christ beside me
Christ to win me
Christ to comfort and restore me
Christ beneath me
Christ above me
Christ in quiet
Christ in danger
Christ in hearts of all that love me
Christ in mouth of friend and stranger

Striving to get to that place will do us no good – we already live there. So enjoy it! Embrace the enfolding love of God Himself. He is the Alpha and the Omega, the Beginning and the End, and everything in between.

God's kind of warfare

Because God's presence is always with us, He is the answer to the spiritual warfare we face. The peace of having Him overshadow our lives gives us a powerful weapon. Many times in Israel's history, God told the people to do unconventional things: sing, march, shout, wait. "You don't need to fight," He whispered to them, "because this isn't about you, it's about Me. I'm not asking you to strive and pull down things, I'm asking you to make room for Me to act."

"The LORD is a man of war; The LORD is His name," Scripture says in Exodus 15:3. We serve a warrior king, and one of the best places to be with Him is on a battlefield, outnumbered by the enemy, and hearing Him laugh in their face. "Is that all you've got?" He chuckles. Hearing the joy of the battle and the heart of God is utterly

> "My defense is of God, who saves the upright in heart."
> Psalm 7:10

incredible. Spiritual warfare is about discovering the majesty of Jesus and the sovereignty of God. It's about an oak tree growing out of the root of our relationship with God – strong, steadfast, powerful, massive.

Our goal as a church must be to facilitate, with the help of the Holy Spirit, the presence of God among us. Church isn't about meetings, it's about worship, making God an offering, and prayer. Everything we do in church must be God-centered. This is temple worship, and God is restoring it to His people.

The Holy Spirit wants to do two things with us: firstly, He intends to get us to a place where we trust God *for* everything, and *with* everything. Secondly, He seeks to bring us to a place where *He* can trust *us*. The Father will always trust what He sees manifested of the Son in our lives ... the inhabitation of Jesus. It's a pleasure to trust God, knowing that His great love will catch you, if even if you fall off the edge of a cliff. This great God will send you out into battle against impossible odds with a seemingly ludicrous battle plan. March around the enemy for seven days and then shout, He'll say, winking at you the whole time. *"Go your way; behold, I send you out as lambs among wolves,"* He says (Luke 10:3). Fortunately, you're a lamb with a Lion as a friend.

God does not send out His children weak and defenseless, but as soldiers who are vulnerable to who He is. When you're truly vulnerable to God, the Lion can walk with the lamb. No enemy will come against you. *"No weapon formed against you shall prosper,"* as was prophesied in Isaiah 54:17. I am completely convinced that there is a place in God where we can

confuse and exhaust the enemy. We can confound him,
making him tear his hair out with frustration because
his attacks only make us stronger in spirit. If he ignores
us, we'll rip him apart. If he attacks, the Lion will
devour him. This is the place in the spirit God is trying
to get us to.

what church can be

In 2 Corinthians 3:7–18, we get a taste of what Paul
thought church could be:

> But if the ministry of death, written and engraved
> on stones, was glorious, so that the children of
> Israel could not look steadily at the face of Moses
> because of the glory of his countenance, which
> glory was passing away, how will the ministry of
> the Spirit not be more glorious? For if the ministry
> of condemnation had glory, the ministry of
> righteousness exceeds much more in glory. For even
> what was made glorious had no glory in this
> respect, because of the glory that excels. For if what
> is passing away was glorious, what remains is
> much more glorious.
>
> Therefore, since we have such hope, we use great
> boldness of speech – unlike Moses, who put a veil
> over his face so that the children of Israel could not
> look steadily at the end of what was passing away.

But their minds were blinded. For until this day the same veil remains unlifted in the reading of the Old Testament, because the veil is taken away in Christ. But even to this day, when Moses is read, a veil lies on their heart. Nevertheless when one turns to the Lord, the veil is taken away. Now the Lord is the Spirit; and where the Spirit of the Lord is, there is liberty. But we all, with unveiled face, beholding as in a mirror the glory of the Lord, are being transformed into the same image from glory to glory, just as by the Spirit of the Lord.

Let's not settle for something as small as what we have defined as revival when there is a larger blessing to be had. We do not have to be like Moses, who put a veil over his face so that his friends and countrymen would not look intently at what was fading away. To this day, when the Mosaic law is read, a spiritual veil separates God from man. This veil, Paul teaches, can only be removed by a love for Jesus Christ. Whenever a person turns to the Lord, the veil is ripped to shreds. *"Where the Spirit of the Lord is, there is liberty,"* Paul wrote. *"But we all, with unveiled face, beholding as in a mirror the glory of the Lord, are being transformed into the same image from glory to glory, just as by the Spirit of the Lord."*

We must keep our eyes focused firmly on the cross. Christians who are only intent on pulling down the strongholds of the enemy have not seen the fuller picture. If they had, they would be instead intent on pulling down the very glory of God into their midst. Satan is not the focus of the Church; the Bridegroom is. The only answer to darkness is to switch the light on, and become so full of Jesus that He fights for us. The glory of God, living in God's presence, and being full of His light must be our preoccupation. We are not seekers of the enemy, we are seekers of God. When God comes to us in power, the enemy comes looking for us! And when he does find us, the enemy comes face-to-face with the One who is with us. A stronghold is pulled down when our intimacy with the Lord intimidates the enemy.

> "A lifestyle of intimacy intimidates the enemy."

With increased passion comes an upgrade in favour. Intimacy, passion, presence, and favour all lead us into a greater experience of the glory of God.

Many churches are faced with the same problem as Moses, where the glory of God is rapidly fading from its face. They are in a season of transition where successes are dwindling – but a new glory of God is about to emerge. What will define the church in the next season is not the usual hallmarks of attendance, facility, budget, equipment, missions' work, or even five-fold giftings. These things have only a partial impact on the work of a church. What will define success in this next time period is the amount of the glory of God that is resting upon His people corporately. As people intent on one thing – God's glory – only attracting Him to our midst will be important.

I don't just want to believe *for* God's presence, I want to believe *in* God's presence. I want to see it, taste it, hear it, smell it, and feel it. I want meetings where, without anyone doing anything, no one can stay standing. I have been privileged to be in meetings where rain has fallen inside the building. Where the power of God is so thick that you worship for hours, and the last sound you hear is an exhausted drummer falling through his kit. I've been in meetings where oil has covered everyone's forehead. Where people have been healed and no-one prayed for them. Where lights have appeared and danced around the room. Meetings where hundreds of people heard the voice of God and no-one spoke. Where money appeared in people's pockets and no-one knew how it got there. Poor people walking out of a service wealthy.

I've had many tastes of God's glory – now I want it to become commonplace. The unity and the glory Paul described can happen in our churches. *"Now the Lord is the Spirit; and where the Spirit of the Lord is, there is liberty. But we all, with unveiled face, beholding as in a mirror the glory of the Lord, are being transformed into the same image from glory to glory, just as by the Spirit of the Lord."* It can happen.

real church, real worship

I cannot overemphasize the importance of returning to temple worship. The Jews of Jesus' time had two different types of worship to engage in. In the synagogue, they could hear the word, receive ministry, and have fellowship. In the temple, worship was about interacting with the presence of God. I think we need both forms of worship in our churches, but perhaps not at the same time. My favourite meetings are the ones where we "waste" a lot of time on God. Two, three, four hours, perhaps stretching into the early hours of morning, just worshiping and magnifying God's name: I love that.

"The instinct to worship is hardly less strong than the instinct to eat."
Dorothy Thompson

To worship is to enter the presence of God. Worship is vital to our spiritual health; that's why you must have a personal plan to worship this year. I encourage you to consider how you want to grow in personal worship. "What's going to change?" "What's my strategy going to be?" "What time am I going to allow?" "What am I going to do this year that I didn't do last year?" A vision without a plan is just wishful thinking.

Worship is a multifaceted thing; there are many different frequencies. *Lamentation*, for example, is the most powerful form of worship, but we rarely talk about it. God loves lamentation because it is the only

form of worship that we can do in the absolute reality
of where we are. We cannot hide anything in
lamentation, and God doesn't ask us to. In our lives,
there are times when our situation is inescapable.
A loved one dies; our grief is powerful and absolute.
We cannot put our issue and feelings aside.

Lamentation is when we step into the very thing that
is bothering us and worship God anyway. It is stepping
into our pain, stepping into the reality of what life is
like for us. *"Though He slay me, yet will I trust Him,"*
as Job said in Job 13:15. "Here I am Lord," a lamenting
worshiper says. "Things are bad, but You are glorious
and I worship You."

Habakkuk, an Old Testament prophet, knew
lamentation well (Habakkuk 3:17–18):

> *Though the fig tree may not blossom,*
> *Nor fruit be on the vines;*
> *Though the labor of the olive may fail,*
> *And the fields yield no food;*
> *Though the flock may be cut off from the fold,*
> *And there be no herd in the stalls –*
> *Yet I will rejoice in the LORD,*
> *I will joy in the God of my salvation.*

Things can be grim, but God is the same. He is as
worthy of worship on our worst day as He is on our
best. Lamentation worship is about two words:

"though" and "yet." Though the trees are not blossoming and the fields are not producing, yet I will rejoice in You. Lamentation is a cold-blooded act of will – pushing our emotion aside and choosing to worship. God, knowing the trust it takes to lament, has an indescribable and indefinable way of coming and being with us when we worship in our most painful moments. It is the most sincere form of adoration that exists, and God loves it and inhabits it.

In worship, we must live in the "yet," not the "though." The heart of a decent relationship with God is to never mind the "though" because there is always the "yet." Though the world crumbles, yet will I worship You. Lamentation isn't about worshiping God to try and trick Him into blessing us; it's about saying, "All of these things are true but I don't care – I still want to worship You. I'm not going to ask for anything, I'm just going to worship."

> "It is in the process of being worshipped that God communicates His presence to men."
> C.S. Lewis

At times, we can't help but live in the "though." Difficult things happen and we struggle to worship. But in the life of a Christian, there is always the "yet." Trust in the "yet." Sing about God's majesty, that though you feel pain, yet you will adore Him. Set your heart to worship no matter your circumstance, no matter the style of worship.

Thanksgiving enables us to enter into His presence.

The truth is that God is always with us, whether we feel Him or not. He is perpetually present. Our emotions are a wonderful bonus, but we live by faith. If we give thanks for His presence in all things, our anticipation will release expectation. It's cool to be thankful.

We *praise* God for who He is. We call up His names and thereby rejoice in His nature. He becomes our focus of appreciation and value. We look to Him and our faces are lightened.

In *adoration*, we express our total delight and confidence in God. Our role in the earth is to be occupied with Jesus. We need to be too busy being fascinated with Him to be intimidated by the enemy. There is a romance, a language of love, a rest in the storm that only comes out of our value to the Father. Adoration flows out of joyful acceptance.

High praise is an adventure. In His presence, we get to reverse the events that consume us by having our attitude and perception joyfully adjusted. In the adversity of life, we can put everything on hold when we deliberately give ourselves to the excitement of involvement with the Holy Spirit in praise.

It is a wonderfully provocative and deeply spiritual experience to deliberately turn your back on a problem in order to face God in exaltation. Lift your eyes and exult in Him. The situation may not have changed but you have become different. What we behold, we become.

Warfare praise is the coolest thing to do when the enemy is present and working. One can stand in front of the enemy and revel in the majesty of God. Warfare is about lifting your eyes above the foe and seeing God, present and happy. It is calling to the One who is more than a conqueror; it brings down His names and exults His sovereignty.

At times, the battleground seems to disappear for me and I am enveloped in the cloud and fragrance of God's glory. Time passes and when the cloud dissipates, so has the enemy.

God is unveiling our faces and removing anything that keeps us from focusing on Him. He is letting us into a holy place we've never seen or experienced. Worship is for life, not just for meetings. You can only give corporately what you are giving individually.

When we discipline ourselves to behold Jesus in every circumstance, a transformation occurs. We learn how to sit, wait, and watch for Him every day. The Holy Spirit teaches us about face-to-face, personal adoration; it comes from a worship that flows from a place of rest. When we sit at Jesus' feet and just be, as Mary did, we behold Him. Worship cannot come out of striving, but out of stillness. Spending time with God gives us a touch from Him – this touch is such a pleasure that it will cause a spirit of adoration to well up in us, and overflow. Jesus isn't looking for Mary to reach up to Him and try to curry favor; He is looking for Mary to simply be with Him, allowing Him to reach down and honor her.

find your peace

Mary knew how to be still. She knew where her peace could be found. In the bustle of her sister's work, Mary knew that to truly enjoy Jesus, she had to step back and simply *be*. One of the fruit of the Spirit listed in Galatians 5:22–23 is self-control. Self-control, in fact, is the only form of control acceptable in church life. Practice taking your thoughts captive and you'll soon find that they won't wander away from God's promises, even on your worst and most potentially anxious days. *"And do not be conformed to this world, but be transformed by the renewing of your mind, that you may prove what is that good and acceptable and perfect will of God,"* Paul wrote in Romans 12:2. It is part of the Holy Spirit's job description to help us transform our minds. Ask Him for help, and He will do just that. He loves the process of bringing us to a place where we live in the *"good and acceptable and perfect will of God."*

When our mind is fixed on God, our heart is fixed on Him. There should be nowhere to go to in your devotional life because you're already there. Enjoy the discipline of being at rest. Devotion should be different from prayer – don't mix the two. Sometimes when we come into our quiet time, we have too much of an agenda: "Pray for this, pray for that, thank You very much." We need to just sit and adore Him, feeling who He is. "Inspire me, Holy Spirit," should be our whisper.

When we sit and worship Him, the Holy Spirit can then move on us and lead us to pray about the people and situations He wants to see changed. We shift from our task list of prayer to His.

> "Worship is giving God the best that He has given you. Take time to meditate before God and offer the blessing back to Him in a deliberate act of worship."
> Oswald Chambers

Throughout the day, how many times do you stand back and worship God?

Take time, even five minutes, to simply worship. It can make a world of difference.

Years ago, I worked for a training company. Often, I would go into my office and ask my secretary to hold my calls for ten minutes. I'd close the door, sit down at my desk, and spend ten minutes adoring Jesus. On really rough days, I'd make it twenty minutes.

On one particularly rotten morning, I was finishing a twenty-minute session. I came out of my office to let my secretary know that I was ready to face calls when I heard her tell someone on the phone, "Oh, you can't disturb him right now, he's worshiping." And she wasn't a Christian! I looked at her, shocked.

"What did you say?" I asked.

"I told them you were worshiping," she replied.

"How did you know?"

"I figured it out," she said. "I know you're a

Christian, and I know that you go into that office stressed and come out totally different."

I took her out for lunch and we talked more about it. I was amazed at what she had picked up, just from observing me. "You went in stressed, you came out peaceful," she told me. "I realized you and God have been getting along in there."

Don't come with things to do until you go into the business of prayer. When it comes to real devotion, come with nothing to do except to sit and learn how to wait, rest and be. Be still. Fill your mind with Jesus. Faith and stillness are sustenance for your spirit, so learn to focus on Jesus. When your mind wanders off-topic, bring it back. Retrain it; it's had years of having its own way. Renewing your spirit and your mind is exciting and has incredible fruit. Worship becomes natural for you and the peace of God wells up in your heart. God's perspective can be seen more quickly. The helmet of salvation, which Paul mentioned in Ephesians 6:10-20, is the rest of God protecting our thought life. Take some time out to discipline your soul in peace and rest.

Psalm 46 is worship that starts with an earthquake:

Therefore we will not fear,
Even though the earth be removed,
And though the mountains be carried into the
* midst of the sea;*

> *Though its waters roar and be troubled,*
> *Though the mountains shake with its*
> *swelling."*

(Psalm 46:2–3)

The psalmist disciplines himself to hear God's voice in the midst of all the shaking and the song ends with a new revelation about God:

> *"Be still, and know that I am God;*
> *I will be exalted among the nations,*
> *I will be exalted in the earth!"*

(Psalm 46:10)

Stillness is a critical part of growing up in the Spirit and truly knowing the presence of God. When the landscape shifts beneath your feet, be still and know He is God.

Immature, or soulish, Christians come into a shaky situation praying, "If it be Your will, Lord." The spirit Christian, however, prays, "Father, I ask You to do this." There's a world of difference in the faith levels of those two prayers. A soulish Christian will pray in hope; a spirit Christian will pray in faith. There is a certainty of God's presence."

> "We only learn to behave ourselves in the presence of God."
> C.S. Lewis

testing your peace

Our circumstances are not the house in which we are called to live spiritually. The name of the Lord is our strong tower and refuge, and we have to discipline ourselves to live there, and not in our issues. Mary ran to the feet of Jesus while Martha lived in the kitchen. If you're enjoying your life at the moment, learn to be happy in the happiness of God. There is a place in God's heart for you. If you're in a time of grief, then let God come and comfort you. Either way, God wants to come to you in what is happening. He may come as your Comforter, wrapping His arms around you and holding you tight, even as you cry into His chest. He may come as your Prince of Peace, calming your emotions. He may come as your King of Joy, laughing and swinging you around. Just come to God as you are.

We live by grace. Good days and bad days don't exist; there are only days of grace. Some days, the grace of God allows you to enjoy life and, other days, endure life. Don't think about good or bad – just think about grace. "I have grace for this, to enjoy it and to have a really good time," or "I have grace for this, to endure it." Find Mary's heart, learning to come, to sit, to be, to wait, to rest, to abide in Jesus. Waiting for God is our age's great discipline. *"But those who wait on the LORD shall renew their strength; they shall mount up with wings like eagles, they shall run and not be weary,*

A prophetic word

Cross over, My children
From all you have known, seen, and tasted of My presence.

For all that has passed before you on the journey of worship
Has been to bring you to this place.

For I am taking the heart of stone
Out of the lives of My people
To free them from selfish restraint and self pre-occupation...
That they may behold Me.

In these days, I will be your reward as you worship
You will enter into that place of adoration
That the angels occupy around My throne.

For it shall be on earth, even as it is in heaven
Worship from the earth shall ascend and meet
Worship descending from heaven
When the first heaven meets the third heaven
In adoration
All that is demonic in the second heaven
Shall be displaced by the weight of glory.

For I shall come down into that place of adoration
As you seat Me on the throne of your passion
When I come, all things will change
I will adorn My bride with My beauty
And make her ready for My intimate embrace.

Cross over, My children
Set your heart to cross over
Into a new land of worship.

Press in, press in
Learn to stand in joy and admiration
Receive the stamina, the discipline, the will
To push your heart forward.

Give yourself, do not withhold
But push, push on, push through
Give birth to a new song
That will captivate your heart as it captivates Mine.

This song will fill the earth
It will fill My house
It will fill My temple
Even as it fills your heart.

A new land awaits you
Go in and possess your possessions.

In worship, in adoration
Receive My longing for you
Let My aching heart refresh you
Replenish you, restore you.

they shall walk and not faint" – this is the promise from Isaiah 40:31 for us.

Why are so many Christians stressed out, tired, anxious, burned out, and living with a negative emotional lifestyle? It is our lack of ability to rest and our inability to live in "day-tight" compartments. We allow yesterday's issues to spill over into the next day. "New every morning" is the promise of God's compassion and lovingkindness. Just as the Israelites were given new manna every morning in the desert, God's mercy is always fresh.

Our experience of God becomes stale when we do not treat each day as new in His presence. What new things may occur if we lived in the newness of life promised to us in Scripture? In Romans 5:1–5, we see the life in Christ that we have been given:

> *Therefore, having been justified by faith, we have peace with God through our Lord Jesus Christ, through whom also we have access by faith into this grace in which we stand, and rejoice in hope of the glory of God. And not only that, but we also glory in tribulations, knowing that tribulation produces perseverance; and perseverance, character; and character, hope. Now hope does not disappoint, because the love of God has been poured out in our hearts by the Holy Spirit who was given to us.*

The apostle Paul knew this concept well. *"The life which I now live in the flesh I live by faith in the Son of God, who loved me and gave Himself for me,"* he wrote in Galatians 2:20. Paul learned how to live from the inside to the outside. He never doubted that God loved him, or was with him. He never wondered if God was listening or if He was speaking. We must follow Paul's example in this.

> "We are so often caught up in our activities that we tend to worship our work, work at our play, and play at our worship."
> Charles Swindoll

God will test your commitment to rest, peace, and adoration. He used the wind and waves to test His disciples, for example, in Mark 4:35–41:

On the same day, when evening had come, He said to them, "Let us cross over to the other side." Now when they had left the multitude, they took Him along in the boat as He was. And other little boats were also with Him. And a great windstorm arose, and the waves beat into the boat, so that it was already filling. But He was in the stern, asleep on a pillow. And they awoke Him and said to Him, "Teacher, do You not care that we are perishing?"

Then He arose and rebuked the wind, and said to the sea, "Peace, be still!" And the wind ceased and there was a great calm. But He said to them, "Why are you so fearful? How is it that you have no faith?"

And they feared exceedingly, and said to one another, "Who can this be, that even the wind and the sea obey Him!"

Jesus knew the storm was brewing and He decided to seize the moment to gauge His disciples' faith. "We'll take the boys for a boat ride and see what they're made of," He thought to Himself. As the waves began to roll, Scripture tells us Jesus was sleeping. I sometimes wonder if maybe He just had His eyes closed and was praying: "Make the waves really big, Father. Let's see what Peter and the lads have in them!"

As the storm raged, the disciples panicked. Some of them were experienced fishermen who had sailed all their lives – things must have been bad for them to get that scared. As they rowed and cowered and hung on for dear life, they looked to the back of the boat. There was their friend, Jesus, asleep. "How can He rest at a time like this?" they thought. "How can you *not* rest at a time like this?" Jesus thought back.

When a storm is howling, it's a perfect time to rest. Practice the presence of God at all times when the storms come against you; you'll realize that it's a perfect opportunity to establish that peace even more. When you rest in God, the wind and the waves cannot touch you. They cannot move you, they cannot hurt you. Resting in God means we are being powered by the internal presence of the Almighty, not the external storm.

spreading your peace

Out of His own rest, Jesus spoke the words the disciples had longed to hear: *"Peace, be still."* That's our job on the earth, to spread the peace God has given us. Every newspaper we read, every television program we watch, is consumed with conflict. Wall-to-wall coverage of war, disaster, and scandal – in a word, conflict. Where are the peacemakers in the midst of it all? Where are the Christians who know how to live at peace in the storm? Where have we vanished to? Out of His peace, Jesus spoke peace.

"Blessed are the peacemakers," Jesus preached in Matthew 5:9, *"for they shall be called sons of God."* There have been times when I have walked into a room and the level of peace and faith has risen. When things are hard and we call extraordinary prayer meetings, I know that I can come, carry my devotion to rest, and see peace grow. Why? It's a simple principle: what you take in with you, comes out and is distributed. If you enter a room with bitterness, bitterness is what you distribute. If you enter a room with peace, peace is what is given away. Whatever is in you comes out. If you're operating soulishly, then you will detract from what God wants to do;

if you're acting in a right spirit, you'll add to what He is doing.

what rest looks like

Rest is a better way to live, but it can cause misconceptions. You can live in such a place of rest that people will accuse you of not caring. It's as if they think that someone can't care unless they're all worked up. But an anxious, fearful person is less likely to get an answer from God than one who is living in rest. God is always close by; *"I will not leave you nor forsake you,"* He promised in Joshua 1:5.

God likes to hide – in fact, He invented the game Hide and Seek. In certain seasons, He will reveal Himself to us; in others, He will hide from us. God only hides because He wants to teach us to look for Him. We all want Him to be manifest in our lives, all the time, but God sometimes wants to hide and draw us deeper into His presence.

> "Come to Me, all you who labor and are heavy laden, and I will give you rest."
> Jesus, Matthew 11:28

If God is hiding from us – but He has also promised to never leave nor forsake us – we can extrapolate one thing: God is hiding in plain sight, teaching us to look for Him in a different way. God is unpredictable but completely consistent. We always know where we are with God because He never changes, but we seldom know what He's going to do next.

God will push you into places where you are not equipped to be. To survive and flourish there, we have but one choice: seek God in a place of rest. Let Him carry us forward. God hasn't called us to do the reasonable, the possible, and the attainable. He has called us to do the outrageously impossible.

quiet times

Quiet times are about to be touched by God in a new and powerful way. We need this shock to our system of doing things; we have been so enslaved by our evangelical mindset that we have tried everything, except rest, to reach out and grasp God. But the true discipline of the spirit is to learn how to be touched by Him – how to sit at His feet, as Mary did, and be loved for simply *being.* If you knew how much God wants to touch you, wants to speak to you, wants to be with you, you would never doubt Him again. If you knew the intensity of God's heart for you, your life would be changed.

The Holy Spirit has many duties and responsibilities, but one of His great pleasures is teaching us how to abide in God. He loves to discipline us in staying, dwelling, and remaining in Him. Transformation takes place when we rest in His everlasting arms. So wait joyfully, knowing that God is about to change you forever.

To have an effective devotional life, we must

understand the difference between the soul and the spirit. In Scripture, the soul – your mind, will and emotions – represents the striving of man to achieve something or be successful at something. The spirit, however, represents God's place of rest and peace within us. *"Abide in Me, and I in you. As the branch cannot bear fruit of itself, unless it abides in the vine, neither can you, unless you abide in Me,"* Jesus said in John 15:4–5. *"I am the vine, you are the branches. He who abides in Me, and I in him, bears much fruit; for without Me you can do nothing."*

Learning how to abide in the power of Jesus is the great challenge facing the Church today. We must learn to live from within; knowing that God isn't out there in space somewhere, but inside us. Praying for the Holy Spirit to come is irrelevant – the Holy Spirit is already here. A spirit man or woman recognizes God's presence and thanks Him for being with them. "Teach me how to wait, to be still, to live by faith," a spirit-led Christian prays. "You said You would never leave us nor forsake us, and I know it to be true. Thank You. How can I serve You?"

> "Bidden or not bidden, God is present."
> Erasmus

conclusion

A call has gone out from Heaven to the Church: learn how to turn and yield within yourself to the presence of

God. This is a discipline we need to practice every day of our lives. It may not come easily, but we must not be discouraged – God is in the beginning, and He will also be there in the end. It doesn't matter where you are or what you feel; God is with you and that's enough. Be faithful and withdraw your heart from outward distractions. Turn away from them and yield to God on the inside. Forget Martha's dishes in the sink, and sit at His feet like Mary did. Form a habit of turning inwardly to God and abide within Him.

Turning and yielding to God refreshes us. We learn how to bounce back when we fail. One of my early mentors watched me grow frustrated as I kept falling into temptation – I was very hard on myself. "Do you know what the best way is to harass the enemy?" he asked me one day.

"Tell me," I said.

"Bounce back from a defeat as quickly as you can," he answered. "Perfect the art of bouncing back and, one day, there will be nothing to bounce back from."

Nothing is more disconcerting for the enemy than seeing you bounce back from a defeat he took so much time to lure you into. The blood of Jesus cleanses all sin – when you bounce back in repentance, it tears down all of the work of the enemy. Sometimes, intimacy with God is blocked by the rubbish within ourselves; if we can change our mind, though, the Holy Spirit will change our emotion. Intimacy with God is about allowing the love of God to come in and displace the rubbish that is present.

God has planted a divine "Yes" in your heart. *"For all the promises of God in Him are Yes, and in Him Amen, to the glory of God through us,"* the Bible says in 2 Corinthians 1:20. Your heart wants to be in that "Yes" place with God.

At the end of the day, it is the loveliness of God that is going to accomplish the promises in your life. Through His goodness, His kindness, His peace, and His joy, He will strengthen you. Learn how to sit and rest and wait and be. Fill your mind with Jesus, and your life will never be the same.

A prayer ...

Father,

>   I pray that I will love You with
>   All my heart today
>   That my mind will dwell in worship
>   On You
>   That my will and emotion (or lack of it) will bend towards
>   adoration
>   Of Jesus
>   That my strength and energy of life will bless
>   And glorify You
>   That every thought and word will give
>   You pleasure
>   That every action of mine this day will make
>   You smile.

Jesus deserves nothing less.

>   In His Name,
>   Amen.

exercise 1:
lamentation

Lamentation is a powerful, and meaningful, form of worship because it places our love for God above even the worst circumstances in our life. No one in Scripture models this form of worship better than Job.

One day, Satan walked into Heaven and had an interesting conversation with God.

"Where have you been?" God asked.

"I've been roaming the earth," the enemy replied.

"Have you noticed Job?" God said proudly. "He is blameless and upright and fears Me like no one else on earth does."

"Of course he does," Satan answered. "You've given him everything. Take it away, and he would curse You to Your face."

"Try it," God said. "Take everything from him but his health, and let's just see what happens."

God gave permission for a season, and the enemy stripped Job of everything he could, even his children. Still, Job stood and blessed God's name.

Satan returned to Heaven and upped the ante. God gave the enemy permission to take Job's health, and still the man stood. It was in the midst of this torment that we see the strength and depth of Job's love for God. *"Though He slay me, yet I will trust Him,"* he lamented in Job 13:15. That line has become the basis for Kevin Prosch's powerful worship song, "Kiss the Son":

> When You've been broken
> Broken to pieces
> And your heart begins to faint
> 'Cause you don't understand
> And when there is nothing
> To reap from the ashes
> And you can't even walk
> Onto the fields of praise
>
> But I bow down and kiss the Son
> Oh I bow down and kiss the Son
>
> When the rock falls
> Falls upon you
> And you get no music for the pain
> You open the windows
> The windows of heaven
> And then you hold me
> And you crush me like a rose
>
> Let the praise of the Lord be in my mouth
> Let the praise of the Lord be in my mouth

Though You slay me I will trust You
Though You slay me I will trust You

Job stood fast, turning his agony into worship. He took everything we have been trained to fear: total disaster, complete ruin, hunger, disaster – even death – and praised the Lord.

God does not ask us to deny the existence of our suffering. He does want us to collect it, stand in those things, and make Him an offering. The Holy Spirit, our Comforter, helps us to do this: He aligns Himself with our will and says, "I will help you to will to worship God." The glory of the majesty of God is that He helps us *will* and *do*.

Too often, we either back away from our grief when we come to worship, or we quit worshiping at all in the face of the pain. We feel like we have to come to Him at our best, highest point. But God's heart is to accept us as we are. He wants us to step into that pain and worship Him with it.

The psalmists understood lamentation as well. In Psalm 42, the writer poured out his heart to God, laying out all of the difficulties he faced:

As the deer pants for the water brooks,
So pants my soul for You, O God.
My soul thirsts for God, for the living God.
When shall I come and appear before God?
My tears have been my food day and night,
While they continually say to me,
"Where is your God?"

When I remember these things,
I pour out my soul within me.
For I used to go with the multitude;
I went with them to the house of God,
With the voice of joy and praise,
With a multitude that kept a pilgrim feast.

Why are you cast down, O my soul?
And why are you disquieted within me?
Hope in God, for I shall yet praise Him
For the help of His countenance.

O my God, my soul is cast down within me;
Therefore I will remember You from the land
*   of the Jordan,*
And from the heights of Hermon,
From the Hill Mizar.
Deep calls unto deep at the noise of Your
*   waterfalls;*
All Your waves and billows have gone
*   over me.*

*The LORD will command His lovingkindness in
   the daytime,
And in the night His song shall be with me –
A prayer to the God of my life.*

*I will say to God my Rock,
"Why have You forgotten me?
Why do I go mourning because of the
   oppression of the enemy?"
As with a breaking of my bones,
My enemies reproach me,
While they say to me all day long,
"Where is your God?"*

*Why are you cast down, O my soul?
And why are you disquieted within me?
Hope in God;
For I shall yet praise Him,
The help of my countenance and my God.*

Lamentation does not deny the existence of pain; it
does just the opposite, in fact. It actually involves
worshiping God with that sorrow. What are the
circumstances of your life? Are you in the winepress of
God, being crushed like a grape? What is the sorrow
you are feeling? If you have none, don't dig it up: just
be blessed and live life to the full.

If you are in mourning, you have the opportunity to
worship in the most powerful way possible:

lamentation. This worship isn't done in order to have God remove the pain. It simply recognizes that God stands in the moment with us. Lamentation elevates God in the presence of our enemies. It brings out a side of God that other forms of worship simply cannot touch.

In this exercise, we will craft our own prayer of lamentation, focusing on two words: "Though" and "Yet." Again, if you are not in a season of grief, rejoice and move on. But for those of you in a season of mourning, try this exercise.

1. Find a quiet place before God. Rest in His glory. Close your eyes. Ask Him to stir up the Holy Spirit He has deposited in you and to draw as near to you as possible.

2. Simply *be*. Just drink in His presence. If your mind begins to wander, bring it back to the wonder of God. Give yourself to Him completely.

3. Take a pen and write down the "Though" circumstances in your life. The challenges you are currently facing, the pain you feel, the grief you haven't shared. Make an offering to God of the things that have wounded you.

Though . . . .
. . . .
. . . .
. . . .

Though . . . .
. . . .
. . . .
. . . .

Though . . . .
. . . .
. . . .
. . . .

Though . . . .
. . . .
. . . .
. . . .

Though . . . .
. . . .
. . . .
. . . .

4. Now rephrase your worship for God. "Though
    these things have happened, yet what will you
    do?" Don't ask Him for anything, simply bless and
    honour Him. Don't let anything stop you from
    exalting Him. Write your promises and worship to
    God in a series of "Yet" statements:

    Yet

    . . . .
    . . . .
    . . . .

Yet

. . . .
. . . .
. . . .

Yet

. . . .
. . . .
. . . .

Yet

. . . .
. . . .
. . . .

Yet I will worship You.

5. Now go back and re-read your "Though" and
   "Yet" statements, as a psalm of lamentation to
   God. Use it to worship God in your quiet time with
   Him. Add and change verses as you deem
   necessary over the next several weeks and months.

exercise 2:
a promise from Ephesians 3:14–21

Ephesians 3:14–21 carry an important piece of the
puzzle of simply resting in God, and becoming more
like Him. Let's read the passage:

> *For this reason I bow my knees to the Father of our
> Lord Jesus Christ, from whom the whole family in
> heaven and earth is named, that He would grant
> you, according to the riches of His glory, to be
> strengthened with might through His Spirit in the
> inner man, that Christ may dwell in your hearts
> through faith; that you, being rooted and grounded
> in love, may be able to comprehend with all the
> saints what is the width and length and depth and
> height – to know the love of Christ which passes
> knowledge; that you may be filled with all the
> fullness of God.*
>
> *Now to Him who is able to do exceedingly
> abundantly above all that we ask or think,
> according to the power that works in us, to Him be
> glory in the church by Christ Jesus to all
> generations, forever and ever. Amen.*

To become rooted and grounded in love, we must immerse ourselves in the love of Christ every day. Jesus' love needs to be so real to us that our minds, our hearts, our heads, our tongues, our hands become conduits of that love of God.

Learning to love as God loves breaks down the issues in our lives. Our poor self-image shifts as we see ourselves as Christ sees us. Our history falls by the wayside without a word of counseling or deliverance. God simply infects us completely. When a Divine outpouring of the love of God comes, there is a displacement of the wounds we currently have.

The best thing we can do to prepare for such a revelation of God's love is to quickly get rid of any grudges and bitterness we have been holding on to.

Take a few moments and pray. Ask God if there is anyone who you hold ill will toward. Be sensible about this; we need to get rid of the things that are keeping us from the promise God has given us.

▶ List their names:

. . . .

. . . .

. . . .

▶ How can you restore those relationships? What steps do you need to take toward forgiveness? Choose to forgive, and ask God to bless those people.

▶ Write a prayer of forgiveness and blessing here:

. . . .
. . . .
. . . .
. . . .
. . . .
. . . .

It may not be possible to see the relationship restored or reconciled. But if it is possible, then you need to go for it, expecting the grace, love and support of the Holy Spirit. If restoration is impossible, write a card with a blessing (do it anonymously, if it helps) and send it to them. Make the blessing substantial and significant.

Forgiveness clears the decks of resentment and opens our hearts to be baptized in God's love. If we do this, His promise to us is concrete: *"You, being rooted and grounded in love, may be able to comprehend with all the saints what is the width and length and depth and height – to know the love of Christ which passes knowledge; that you may be filled with all the fullness of God."* God is able to do far more than anything we can think to ask; *"Eye has not seen, nor ear heard, nor have entered into the heart of man the things which God has prepared for those who love Him,"* as Paul wrote in 1 Corinthians 2:9. God's power of love wants to work in you and redeem the time that has been wasted.

The Holy Spirit is calling all of us to learn to live in the outrageous goodness of the majesty of the love of God. He wants us to move in such love that no one is safe from receiving a blessing from God – on the streets, in the coffee shops, on the highways and byways. The love that we carry, birthed out of a Mary-like, restful, intimate relationship with Jesus, can change any situation in a heartbeat.

God wants us to fully engage with Him in this season, because He intends to fully engage with us. It is a time to be whole-hearted in our affection for God, and becoming the son or daughter we were always meant to be.

exercise 3:
lectio divina

Lectio Divina (Latin for Divine Reading) is an ancient way of reading the Bible – allowing a quiet and contemplative way of coming to God's Word. Lectio Divina opens the pulse of the Scripture, helping readers dig far deeper into the Word than normally happens in a quick glance-over.

In this exercise, we will look at a portion of Scripture and use a modified Lectio Divina technique to engage it. This technique can be used on any piece of Scripture; I highly recommend using it for key Bible passages that the Lord has highlighted for you, and for anything you think might be an inheritance word for your life (see the *Crafted Prayer interactive journal* for more on inheritance words).

Psalm 46

God is our refuge and strength,
A very present help in trouble.
Therefore we will not fear,
Even though the earth be removed,

And though the mountains be carried into the
        midst of the sea;
Though its waters roar and be troubled,
Though the mountains shake with its swelling.

                                        Selah

There is a river whose streams shall make glad the
        city of God,
The holy place of the tabernacle of the Most High.
God is in the midst of her, she shall not be moved;
God shall help her, just at the break of dawn.
The nations raged, the kingdoms were moved;
He uttered His voice, the earth melted.

The Lord of hosts is with us;
The God of Jacob is our refuge.

                                        Selah

Come, behold the works of the Lord,
Who has made desolations in the earth.
He makes wars cease to the end of the earth;
He breaks the bow and cuts the spear in two;
He burns the chariot in the fire.

Be still, and know that I am God;
I will be exalted among the nations,
I will be exalted in the earth!

The Lord of hosts is with us;
The God of Jacob is our refuge.

                                        Selah

1. Find a place of stillness before God. Embrace His peace. Calm your body, breathe slowly ... clear your mind of the distractions of life. Ask God to reveal His rest to you. Whisper the word, "Stillness." This can take some time, but once you're in that place of rest, enjoy it. Worship God out of it.

2. Read the passage twice, slowly.

    a. Allow its words to become familiar to you, and sink into your spirit. Picture the scene – become part of it. Listen for pieces that catch your attention.

    b. Following the reading, meditate upon what you have heard. What stands out? Write it down:

        . . . .
        . . . .
        . . . .
        . . . .
        . . . .

    c. If a word or phrase from the passage seems highlighted to you, write it down:

        . . . .
        . . . .
        . . . .
        . . . .
        . . . .

3. Read the passage twice, again.

   a. Like waves crashing onto a shore, let the words of the Scripture crash onto your spirit? What are you discerning? What are you hearing? What are you feeling? Write it down:

      . . . .
      . . . .
      . . . .
      . . . .

   b. What is the theme of this passage? Write it down:

      . . . .
      . . . .
      . . . .
      . . . .

   c. Does this passage rekindle any memories or experiences? Write it down:

      . . . .
      . . . .
      . . . .
      . . . .

   d. What is the Holy Spirit saying to you? Write it down:

      . . . .
      . . . .
      . . . .
      . . . .

4. Read the passage two final times.

    a. Meditate on it.

    b. Is there something God wants you to do with
       this passage? Is there something He is calling
       you to? Write it down:

    . . . .

    . . . .

    . . . .

    . . . .

    c. Pray silently. Tell God what this Scripture is
       leading you to think about. Ask Him for His
       thoughts. Write down your conversation – as if
       you and God are sitting in a coffee shop, two
       old and dear friends, sharing:

    . . . .

    . . . .

    . . . .

    . . . .

5. Pray and thank God for what He has shared with
   you. Come back to the passage a few more times
   over the coming weeks.

FAQ:
frequently asked questions

Q. Who is Graham Cooke and how can I find more information about him?

A. Graham Cooke is a speaker and author who splits his time between Southampton, England, and Vacaville, California. He has been involved in prophetic ministry since 1974. He founded and directed The School of Prophecy, which has received international acclaim for its advanced series of in-depth training programs. Graham is a member of Community Church in Southampton (UK), and is part of c.net (Cornerstone) team. He is married to Heather, and they have three children, Ben, Seth and Sophie. You can learn more about Graham at www.grahamcooke.com or by writing him, PO Box 91, Southampton, England, SO15 57E.

Q. How can I become a prayer partner with Graham?

A. Check his website, www.grahamcooke.com, for all of the information you need.

Q. Has Graham written any other books?

A. Graham has written two other books, *A Divine Confrontation ... Birth Pangs of the New Church* and *Developing Your Prophetic Gifting.* Both are available at most Christian bookstores or at www.grahamcooke.com. Graham has also written three interactive journals, *The Nature of God, Hiddenness and Manifestation*, and *Crafted Prayer.* These are only available from Sovereign World (www.sovereign-world.org) or at www.grahamcooke.com.

about the author

Graham Cooke is married to Heather, and they have three adult offspring, Ben, Seth, and Sophie. Graham and Heather divide their time between Southampton, England, and Vacaville, California.

Graham is a member of the apostolic team of c.net (Cornerstone), a network of ministries and a family of churches spanning 44 nations. He is a member of Community Church in Southampton (UK), responsible for the prophetic and training program, and working with team leader Billy Kennedy. In California, he is part of the pastoral leadership team, working with senior pastor David Crone. He has responsibility for Insight, a training program within the church and for the region.

Graham is a popular conference speaker and is well known for his training programs on the prophetic, spiritual warfare, intimacy with God, leadership, and spirituality. He functions as a consultant within c.net (and beyond), specifically helping churches make the transition from one dimension of calling to a higher level of vision and ministry. He has a passion to build prototype churches that can fully reach our postmodern society.

A strong part of Graham's ministry is in producing finances and resources to help the poor, supporting many projects around the world. He also financially supports and helps to underwrite church planting, leadership development, evangelism, and health and rescue projects in the third world. If you wish to become a financial partner for the sake of missions, please contact Graham's office where his personal assistant, Carole Shiers, will be able to assist you.

Graham has many prayer partners who play a significant part in his ministry. For more information, check his website.

Graham has written two books, *A Divine Confrontation ... Birth Pangs of the New Church* and *Developing Your Prophetic Gifting,* and three interactive journals, *The Nature of God, Hiddeness and Manifestation,* and *Crafted Prayer.*

Contact details for Graham Cooke:

- **United States**: Vaca Valley Christian Life Center, 6391 Leisure Town Road, Vacaville, CA 95687, USA
  email: FUTURETRAININGINST@prodigy.net

- **United Kingdom**: Sword of Fire Ministries, PO Box 1, Southampton, SO16 7WJ
  email: admin@swordfire.org.uk

- **Canada**: Jenny Bateman, Friends at Langley Vineyard, 5708 Glover Road, Langley, BC, V3A 4H8
  email: jenn@shopvineyard.com

- *Website*: http://www.grahamcooke.com